★ IT'S MY STATE! ★
New York

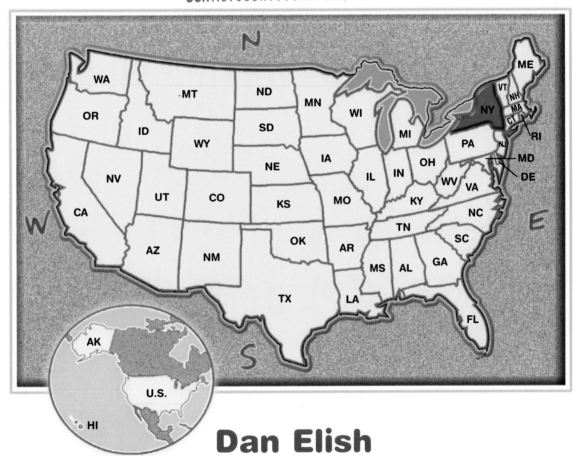

Dan Elish

BENCHMARK BOOKS

MARSHALL CAVENDISH
NEW YORK

Series Consultant

David G. Vanderstel, Ph.D., Executive Director, National Council on Public History

With thanks to Joseph Meany, Ph.D., Acting State Historian of New York, for his expert review of this manuscript.

Benchmark Books
Marshall Cavendish
99 White Plains Road
Tarrytown, New York 10591-9001
www.marshallcavendish.com

Elish, Dan.
New York / by Dan Elish.
p. cm. — (It's my state!)
Summary: Surveys the history, geography, government, and economy of
the Empire State, as well as the diverse ways of life of its people.
ISBN 0-7614-1419-3
1. New York (State)—Juvenile literature. [1. New York (State)] I.
Title. II. Series.
F119.3 .E37   2003   974.7—dc21   2001008371

Photo research by Candlepants, Inc.

Cover Photo: *Photo Researchers, Inc.*, Andy Levin

Back cover illustration: The license plate shows New York's postal abbreviation, followed by its year of statehood.

The photographs in this book are used by permission and through the courtesy of: *Animals Animals-Earth Scenes*: Eastcott/Momatiuk, 4 (top); Ken Cole, 4 (middle); Robert Lubeck, 5 (top), 16; Gregory Brown, 5 (middle); Gary W. Griffen, 14 (bottom); Michael Bisceglie, 15 (top). *Corbis*: Bill Ross, 4 (bottom); Michael Neveux, 5 (bottom); Peter Finger, 9, 49 (bottom), 64; Michael S. Yamashita, 10; Richard Hamilton Smith, 12; D. Robert Franz, 14 (top); Pat O'Hara, 15 (bottom); 18, 24, 45 (low); Bettmann, 21, 29, 30, 32, 33, 37, 44(top), 45 (middle); AFP, 35; Joseph Sohm/Chromosohm, Inc., 38; David Katzenstein, 40; Richard T. Nowitz, 41, 68; Mitchell Gerber, 44 (low); Leif Skoogfors, 45 (top); Farrell Grehan, 50; Lee Snider, 58. 67 (bottom); Owen Franken, 65; Joseph Sohm/ Visions of America, 66 (bottom); Catherine Karnow, 67 (top); Kit Kittle, 70; David Muench, 73. *Photo Researchers, Inc.*: Ellen Young, 8; Frederica Georgia, 13; Paul J. Fusco, 15; Michael P. Gadomski, 15; Vanessa Vick, 17; Ellen B. Senisis, 46; David M. Grossman, 52; Patricia Caulfield, 54; Richard T. Nowitz, 66 (middle); Ken Cavenaugh, 67 (middle); Gerard Smith, 71. *The Bridgeman Art Library/National Gallery of Art, Washington D.C.*: George Catlin, "DeTonty Suing Indians for peace in an Iroquois village," 20. *National Archives of Canada*: (#c-092414) 22. *New York Public Library, Astor Lennox and Tilden Foundation*: Spencer Collection, 23; Print Collection, Mirium & Ira D. Wallach Division of Art Prints and Photographs, 26 (top). Collection of the *New York Historical Society*: 26(low). *Getty Images/* FPG: VCG, 37. *Getty Images/Tony Stone*; Hiroyuki Matsumoto, 42; Dugald Bremner, 49 (top). *N.Y.S. Department of Economic Development 2002*: 53, 56, 62, 66 (top). *Alice Garrard*: 75.

Book design by Anahid Hamparian

Printed in Italy
1   3   5   6   4   2

Contents

A Quick Look at New York

Nickname: The Empire State
Population: 18,976,457 (2000)
Statehood: 1788

Tree: The Sugar Maple

Known primarily for producing the sap that makes maple syrup, the sugar maple is also one of the world's most beautiful trees. Each fall its changing leaves paint the New York landscape in brilliant shades of gold, orange, and red.

Bird: The Bluebird

Handsome and tuneful, the bluebird was made the state bird in 1970. Many people hang special nesting boxes on fences for bluebirds, which winter throughout the state.

Flower: The Rose

Beautiful and fragrant but with a touch of danger (those thorns!), the rose was made the state flower in 1955. Ever popular, the rose was voted the favorite flower by school children in 1891.

Animal: The Beaver

Though only adopted as the state animal in 1975, the beaver played an important part in New York's history. In the 1600s, fur traders bartered with Indians for beaver pelts, which they sold to European merchants. This led many traders to settle near Albany, now the state's capital.

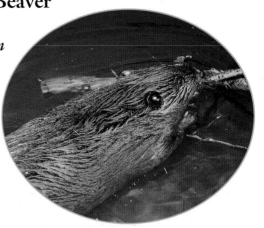

Fish: The Trout

Found in the lakes of the Adirondack Mountains as well as in hundreds of streams throughout the state, the trout was named the New York State fish in 1975.

Beverage: Milk

Since dairy is one of New York's most important industries, it made sense for the legislature to name milk the state beverage in 1981. It takes about two days for a quart of New York milk to get from the cow (where it comes out at 101 degrees!) to the grocery store.

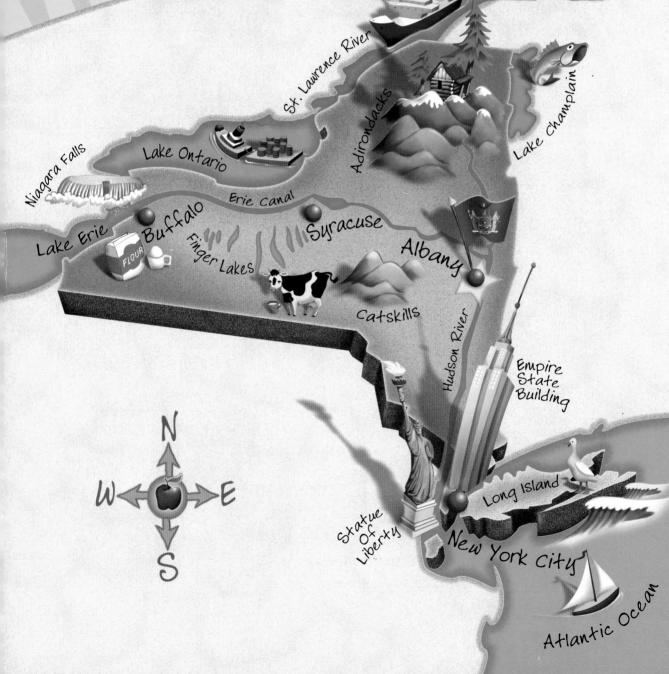

NEW YORK

St. Lawrence River

Niagara Falls

Lake Ontario

Lake Champlain

Adirondacks

Lake Erie

Erie Canal

Buffalo

Finger Lakes

Syracuse

Albany

FLOUR

Catskills

Hudson River

Empire State Building

N
W E
S

Statue Of Liberty

Long Island

New York City

Atlantic Ocean

1 The Empire State

During the height of the American Revolution, General George Washington toured New York colony and declared that it would one day become the seat of an empire. Though the "Empire State" was a land of forests and mountains, America's first president knew what he was talking about. A century later New York City had become a financial center of North America, and upstate lumberjacks and farmers kept pace producing timber and raising livestock and crops.

Today, New York is home to close to 19 million people, making it the third most populous state in the nation behind California and Texas. It's not quite an "empire," but New York's unique blend of big cities, thriving suburbs, and quiet countryside have turned it into a dynamic state.

The Landscape

Driving on the bustling avenues of New York City or along the quiet roads upstate, it's hard to imagine that the landscape was formed more than one million years ago during a period known as the Ice Age. That's when a huge glacier, towering higher than the Empire State Building, moved across the state and carved out the Finger Lakes, the Hudson River Valley, and the

7

valleys of the Adirondacks. It also created Long Island.

At 49,576 square miles, New York is the thirtieth largest state in America and is often divided into seven regions. Hugging the Saint Lawrence River in the northeastern section of the state, lies the flat terrain and rich soil of the Saint Lawrence Lowland. Farther south, the majestic Adirondack

A boy explores the wonder of New York's great outdoors.

Mountains rise in a region called the Adirondack Upland. This is wonderful "outdoors" country, where New Yorkers can take peaceful walks along wooded trails or hike to a mountaintop for a stunning view. Mount Marcy, at 5,344 feet, is New York's highest peak.

The family farm is one of the state's most enduring industries.

South of the Adirondacks lies the Hudson-Mohawk Lowland with some of the most fertile farmland in the country. The Hudson and Mohawk Rivers flow through the region. Winding country roads, solitary creeks, and small farms and towns dot this part of the state. The New England Upland sits to the east of the Hudson River along the Taconic Mountains, while the Atlantic Coastal Plain stretches across the southeastern section of the state. This region includes Long Island and the state's beachfront property, along Long Island Sound and the Atlantic Ocean.

The Appalachian Plateau is the largest of the Empire State's seven regions. The Finger Lakes and some of New York's most lovely scenery are here. Known for its flat expanses and beautiful snowy winters, this region has small towns and dairy farms but few cities. The Great Lakes Lowland fills most

Niagara Falls is actually two waterfalls: the American Falls in New York and the Horseshoe Falls on the Canadian side. The American Falls alone are 1,000 feet wide and drop 176 feet!

of the northwestern section of the state. This is where Lake Oneida is found, as well as three of the state's major cities: Syracuse, Rochester, and Buffalo. The beautiful islands of Lakes Erie and Ontario also lie in this region, not to mention one of the most astounding natural wonders in all of America: Niagara Falls.

> *We'll take Manhattan*
> *The Bronx and Staten Island, too!*
> *It's lovely going to—the zoo.*
>
> **—Richard Rodgers and Lorenz Hart, one of the great songwriting teams of the 20th Century**

The Five Boroughs of New York City

Set in the southeastern corner of the state, New York City, otherwise known as the Big Apple, is not set on one piece of land. Rather, it is a collection of five boroughs connected by roads, bridges, and tunnels. The island of Manhattan is 13.4 miles long and 2.3 miles wide. This is where you can find the Wall Street business district, Central Park, and the glittering lights of Times Square. A nine-mile strait known as the East River separates Manhattan from Long Island. On the western tip of Long Island are the boroughs of Queens and Brooklyn, a borough so large that it once had its own professional baseball team, the Dodgers. The Bronx, located across the Harlem River from Manhattan, is the only borough actually on the United States' mainland. Finally, across Upper New York Bay, a short ferry ride from lower Manhattan, lies Staten Island.

Walter P. Chrysler, president of Chrysler Corporation, once said that he wanted to build "a bold structure, declaring the glories of the modern age." The result was the Chrysler Building.

A hiker takes in Rainbow Falls in the Adirondacks.

Climate

New York State has an extremely varied climate. The people of western New York, from Syracuse through Rochester and Buffalo, experience harsh winters like those of northern Canada. More than 100 inches of snow can fall each season. Not that winter is a picnic for those New Yorkers who live farther south. As one native New Yorker put it, "There's nothing worse than rounding a street corner in the city in January and getting hit head on by a blast of wind. Talk about cold!" And the Adirondacks? Years ago they were nicknamed America's Siberia.

Of course, New York does have more temperate seasons. The crisp air of autumn comes to the state in early September and generally lingers into early November. New York is located far enough south that spring comes relatively early. Temperatures are moderate through mid-June. Summers, too, can be extremely pleasant—if you're lucky enough to live upstate or in the mountains. July and August in New York City, however, can be hot and humid, with daytime temperatures in the upper nineties.

Plants & Animals

Bald Eagle

Once nearly extinct in the lower forty-eight states, bald eagles are making a comeback in the Empire State. In the year 2000 alone, there were 350 sightings! A 73-mile stretch along the Delaware River was the hot spot, where 145 eagles were seen.

Pigeon

In terms of animal life, New York City is known mostly for its pigeons. Though sometimes referred to as rats with wings, they make a charming sight pecking for bread in the park or loitering on apartment windowsills. It's hard to imagine the Big Apple without them.

Deer

Due to conservation efforts and limited hunting seasons, there are now more deer in New York State than when the first settlers landed on Plymouth Rock! These days, running across a small herd of white-tailed deer is commonplace in most rural and suburban areas.

Moose

Nearly 100,000 acres of land were purchased by New York State and set aside as a wildlife management area. As a result, in 1980, after an absence of more than one hundred years, moose were once again sighted in the state.

Goldenrod

Each spring, goldenrod grows along New York's trails, roads, and clearings, often flowering next to wild asters and deep violet ironweed.

Buttercup

Buttercups decorate New York State's many fields and pastures. In the words of L.M. Montgomery, "Like showers of gold dust on the marsh . . . the buttercups are dancing now . . ."

Wildlife

Over the past four hundred years New York City has been transformed from a small green island into one of the most awe-inspiring cement landscapes in the world. Nothing can quite match the thrill of driving over one of the city's many bridges and seeing the glorious sweep of the Manhattan skyline.

> *The city seen from the Queensboro Bridge is always the city seen for the first time, in its first wild promise of all the mystery and beauty in the world.*
>
> —F. Scott Fitzgerald, American novelist

Of course, there are stunning views throughout the state that aren't made of concrete! New York has 8,000 lakes and about 150 kinds of trees. More than 60 percent of the land is covered by forest, and the state is teeming with 97 species of mammals, 455 species of birds, and 400 species of fish.

New York has set aside some wonderful places to see all this spectacular wildlife. Located on the southeastern shore of Lake Ontario, the Derby Hill Bird Observatory is one of America's best bird-watching sites. More than 18,000 broad-winged hawks have been known to soar overhead on a single April day. The Lime Hollow Nature

Many black bears live in New York's forests

A group of Brooklyn third graders learn about their state's environment.

Center, two miles from the city of Cortland, offers views of Canada geese, mallards, and wood ducks. Closer to New York City is the Mashomack Preserve. Making up one-third of Shelter Island at the eastern end of Long Island, this area is home to one of the densest populations of breeding ospreys on the East Coast.

New York's natural world is managed by an organization called the Bureau of Wildlife. Founded by the state legislature in 1895 at a time when wildlife populations were extremely small, the bureau's mission is to protect New York's animal life. Due to its efforts, species such as the beaver, white-tailed deer, wood duck, bald eagle, peregrine falcon, ruffed grouse, and wild turkey have been brought back from the brink of extinction and are now often seen in New York forests, fields, and waterways. This means that New Yorkers can icefish in January, watch for flocks of robins in March, spy a wild turkey feeding by hayfields in August, observe the southward flight of the monarch butterfly in September, or catch a glimpse of an antlered buck deer on a fine October day.

No doubt about it: there is more to New York than busy cities. One of the Empire State's greatest assets is its animal life.

A boy waits for his next customer at a shoe-shine stand in early-twentieth-century New York City.

2 From the Beginning

The story goes that in 1624 one of the state's early settlers, a Dutchman named Peter Minuit, bought the island of Manhattan for the Dutch West India Company from a Native American for twenty-four dollars! If true, it was undoubtedly one of the greatest real-estate bargains in history—for New York City has become one of the most valuable pieces of land in the world. Though not all of the decisions made by the settlers of New York have been this profitable, many other New Yorkers have changed the course of history.

Early Settlers

Ten thousand years ago New York State was populated by hunters who tracked herds of elk and caribou, caught bears, fish, and small mammals, and gathered plants and seeds from the forest. In fact, archaeologists continue to discover spearheads and stone knives left by those first New Yorkers.

Still, the first documented history of the state begins with the Native Americans—the true discoverers of America whom Christopher Columbus incorrectly called Indians. Initially, several tribes of Algonquian-speaking people populated New York. They lived along the banks of the lower Hudson River and on

European explorers meet with the Iroquois in 1680. Painting by George Catlin.

present-day Staten Island, Long Island, and Manhattan until the Mohawk, Oneida, Onondaga, Cayuga, and Seneca tribes moved south from the forests upstate and overcame them. These five tribes waged fierce wars among themselves until about 1570, when they formed the Iroquois Confederacy. This was a political organization in which each tribe enjoyed some independence but answered to the authority of the Great Council. Most important, the tribes agreed to fight as one and not against each other. At the height of its power, the Iroquois Confederacy dominated the New York and Lake Erie region.

Legend has it that Hiawatha, a member of the Onondaga tribe, joined forces with a mysterious outsider called Deganawida, or the Peacemaker, and together they convinced the warring tribes of upstate New York to unite and form the Iroquois Confederacy.

Father Isaac Jogues was a French Catholic missionary who lived among the American Indians. He wrote in 1643:

On the island of Manhatte, and its environs [surrounding area], there may well be four or five hundred men of different sects and nations. The Director General [Governor] told me that there were men of eighteen different languages. They are scattered here on the river, as the beauty and convenience of the spot invited each to settle.

"When I came on shore [of New York Bay], the . . . natives all stood around and sung in their fashion; . . . They cook by baking, and it is excellent eating."
—Henry Hudson, 1609

The Europeans

The written history of New York begins in 1524 when an Italian explorer, Giovanni da Verrazano, sailed into what is now the harbor of New York City. Later he wrote: "They [a tribe of Algonquins] came toward us very cheerfully, making great sounds of admiration, showing us where we might come to land most safely with our boat." He also noted what many other new arrivals to New York City throughout the years have thought: "It seemed so commodious and delightful, and which we supposed must contain great riches."

Though Verrazano soon sailed back to Europe, other explorers followed in search of those riches. In 1608 a Frenchman, Samuel de Champlain, discovered what is now known as Lake Champlain in the northeastern part of the state. The following year he set up a fur-trading post near Quebec, Canada. Also in 1609, Henry Hudson, an Englishman employed by the Dutch, sailed up the river that now bears his name as far as what is now Albany.

In 1624, the Dutch had set up a post in what they called Fort

Orange (present-day Albany). That same year Peter Minuit bought the island the natives called Man-a-hat-ta. By 1660, the Dutch had formed a small community at the southern tip of the island of Manhattan, which they called New Amsterdam. On the northern border of the town stood a wall to keep out Indians that was later replaced by a wall known as Wall Street. Up north on Manhattan was a farming community called Nieuw (now Harlem) and across the East River was Breuckelen (now Brooklyn). Across the Harlem River a village grew around a farm owned by Jonas Bronck (now the Bronx, one of New York City's five boroughs).

But events in Europe soon intruded on the peaceful Dutch community. War broke out between England and the Netherlands. In 1664, the British sailed into New York Harbor. The Dutch governor, Peter Stuyvesant, seeing he was hopelessly outnumbered, surrendered immediately. Soon afterward, King Charles II of England gave the new land to his brother, the duke of York, as a gift, and the province was named New York after him.

This leader of the Iroquois Confederacy was received by Queen Anne at the British court in 1710.

The British were gracious victors, however, and allowed the Dutch to remain in their homes. Soon Dutch, French, German, and British colonists were arriving at the new port.

The American Revolution and Beyond

By the mid-1700s, thirteen colonies stretched along the Atlantic seaboard from Georgia to what is now Maine. Throughout that era, the British and French fought the French and Indian Wars over the right to control the North American fur trade. Due in large part to the help of the powerful Iroquois, the British were victorious in 1763. But wars are expensive. To get some money quickly, the British government decided to tax the American colonies. This was a fateful mistake.

Though colonists remained loyal to the British king, many others were in no mood to pay for Britain's wars. Tensions built. "Taxation without representation!" became the cry of the day. By 1775 the colonies were at war with Britain for their independence. But New York lay directly between the southern and northern New England colonies. Due to the state's geographical position, Britain's strategy was to occupy

British warships get ready for battle near Staten Island during the Revolutionary War.

The Battle of Saratoga. Every September visitors to Saratoga Springs, New York, can go back in time to 1777 and watch a re-creation of the battle that was fought there.

it and in that way separate the northern colonies from the rest of the young country. As a result, nearly one-third of the war's battles were fought in the Empire State. The most important battle, often called the turning point of the American Revolution, was at Saratoga in 1777. The British lost, and immediately afterward the French joined the war on the American side.

When the war was finally over and the new country called the United States of America was established, a state agency called the New York Land Board bought most of the land in western New York from the Iroquois and sold it off at low prices to white settlers. Many New Englanders jumped at the chance, and soon new towns called Hudson, Ithaca, Syracuse, and Buffalo sprang up in the western and northern sections of the state.

Unfortunately, the War of 1812 turned parts of New York

back into a battlefield once more as British troops attacked and burned Fort Niagara and parts of Buffalo. New York was also the scene of Commodore Thomas Macdonough's decisive victory in the Battle of Lake Champlain near Plattsburgh. Not until the signing of the Treaty of Ghent in 1814 was the war over and New Yorkers free to get back to the business of building their communities and bringing industry to all parts of the state. By 1820, about 1,400,000 people lived in New York, making it the most populated state in the country.

The Erie Canal

In the early 1800s, the people of New York realized that if a canal could be built connecting the Atlantic Ocean and the Great Lakes, it would create economic opportunity for New York and forge a link between the eastern United States and the Midwest. Though DeWitt Clinton, the mayor of New York City and later governor of the state, was especially enthusiastic about the idea, most people thought it couldn't be done. "It is a splendid project and may be executed a century hence," said Thomas Jefferson, our third president. "But it is a little short of madness to think of it at this day!"

Nonetheless, Clinton finally convinced the New York State legislature to grant seven million dollars for the project. Work on "Clinton's ditch" began in 1817. Due to the back-breaking labor of thousands of workers, it was completed eight years later. In the end, the canal ran 363 miles from Albany on the Hudson River to Buffalo on the shore of Lake Erie. As hoped, the canal successfully connected the Great Lakes to the Hudson River and New York City—and helped jumpstart northwestern New York's economy.

The men who built the Erie Canal had their work cut out for them. The canal stretches hundreds of miles through forests and swamps.

This song, perhaps America's most famous work anthem, was sung by laborers as they dug the Erie Canal.

I've got a mule, her name is Sal, Fifteen miles on the Erie Canal. She's a good ol' worker and a good ol' pal, Fifteen miles on the Erie Canal.

A boat navigates the Erie Canal at Little Falls, New York.

The Civil War

The most troubling issue the American people had to face in the first eighty years of their history was slavery. Since the time the British first established colonies in the New World, southern plantation owners relied on black slaves to work in their fields. At the same time, most northerners felt strongly that slavery was morally wrong. In 1861, years of tension between the North (the Union) and the South (the Confederacy) finally exploded into the Civil War.

Most New Yorkers were abolitionists, men and women who believed that slavery should be ended, or abolished. Even so, when President Abraham Lincoln signed the Enrollment Act of 1863, a bill that established a draft into the army, many citizens were furious. With news of the grisly battle at Gettysburg on the front page of the major papers, Lincoln's call for 300,000 more soldiers frightened even those people who believed in the cause. Further, many poor people, Irish immigrants in particular, were angry that for three hundred dollars wealthy citizens could buy their way out of service. The result was the New York City draft riots. For three days in July of 1863, mobs swarmed through the city's streets, protesting the war by looting stores and burning buildings. Tragically, some rioters took out their frustrations on innocent black Americans. An orphan home built to house African-American children was burned. Union troops were pulled from battle to help restore order.

Despite the horror of the draft riots, New York State and its citizens ultimately rallied to the Union cause. In fact, by the war's end in 1865, New York State had supplied more munitions, paid more taxes, and contributed more to relief efforts than any other state. The Empire State also supplied more than forty generals and close to a half a million troops. Fifty thousand New Yorkers died on Civil War battlefields.

Industrialization

In the mid-1800s America entered a period known as the Industrial Revolution, when new technologies made it easier for manufacturers and industries to produce goods on a large scale. Business boomed. Buffalo became the home of many steel plants. Railroad tracks were laid down throughout the state, connecting cities and towns. The first New York City elevated railway—or "El"—opened for business in 1870.

At the same time, a new generation of businessmen began to make their mark on American industry. In New York City, a man named Isaac Singer invented the sewing machine. Soon his factories were producing them by the hundreds. In Yonkers, Elisha Graves Otis started a company that made electric elevators for high-rise buildings. In Rochester, a bank teller named George Eastman invented and mass produced the first hand-held camera, the famous "Eastman Kodak." John D. Rockefeller established Standard Oil and was soon the wealthiest person in America.

But successful businesses needed a vibrant workforce. Technological advances in industry coincided with the first big wave of German and Irish immigrants—men and women who came to the United States in search of a better life. Though most of these new Americans found work, it was usually in "sweatshops," factories where the owners wanted as many goods made as quickly as possible at the expense of safe and clean working conditions. There was no forty-hour week, minimum wage, or

A family of immigrants arrives at Ellis Island.

workman's compensation. Young children worked twelve-hour days. The rich grew richer, while by 1900 over 1.5 million immigrants were living in slums. Though the human toll was great, New York State grew enormously in the forty years after the Civil War. By 1890, New York was accounting for a stunning one-sixth of the nation's manufacturing. The most important industries were men and women's clothing, milled flour, machine shop products, textiles, and published materials.

The thing that impressed then as now about New York . . . those who ultimately dominated were so very strong, and the weak so very, very weak— and so very, very many.

—Theodore Dreiser, American novelist

Two girls sit on a tenement stairway in a New York City slum, 1890.

Early Twentieth Century

New York raced into the twentieth century with a roar. In 1898, Manhattan officially joined with Brooklyn, The Bronx, Queens, and Staten Island, increasing New York City's area ten times and almost doubling its population (to three and a half million citizens). Now it was the second largest city in the world after London. Business continued to thrive. Soon the New York Stock Exchange was trading millions of dollars worth of shares a day. The famous Manhattan skyline—rows of skyscrapers— began to take shape. But while industrialists built giant mansions, the slums continued to grow. New York was a state of great wealth and achievement as well as great poverty and need.

Luckily, New Yorkers were smart enough to elect Al Smith as their governor. Serving twice, from 1919 to 1920 and then again from 1923 until 1928, Smith channeled money into public programs for parks, highways, and bridges. He also instituted labor laws to protect workers—including children. Despite Smith's great achievements, there was trouble ahead for New York and America.

In 1929, the entire country was hit by the Great Depression. Many people lost their jobs. Then state Governor—and soon to be president of the United States in 1933—Franklin Delano Roosevelt passed the Temporary Emergency Relief Administration in 1931, the first law in the nation that gave state aid to cities and towns.

Once he was president, Roosevelt continued where he had left

> *New York life among the poor has one central . . . feature—namely, the fact that all live in tenements or in a house built on much the same principle. . . . In the typical tenement house the staircase passes up a well in the center of the house. It has no light from the open air . . . it is absolutely dark at midday.*
>
> —Charlotte O'Brien, Irish American author, 1884.

off, creating what he called the New Deal, a series of public works programs designed to give aid and jobs to Americans who had been hit hardest by the depression. Recovery was slow, but Roosevelt's policies helped New Yorkers dig themselves out of one of the most difficult periods in their history.

A family in Albany County, New York, suffering from poverty and ill health, 1936

World War II and Beyond

In 1941 the United States went to war. New York State did its share in the massive effort to defeat the governments of Germany, Japan, and Italy. The Brooklyn Navy Yard became the largest naval shipyard in the world and the New York Port sent 1,460 convoys (fleets of ships) to the war fronts. About 3 million men and millions of tons of equipment were soon shipped overseas from the Empire State. When peace came, the entire country experienced an enormous economic boom. New

World War II is over! Americans gather to celebrate in Manhattan's Times Square.

York did too. Companies such as IBM and Xerox set up shop upstate and were soon on their way to becoming industrial giants. At the same time, blacks from the south and men and women from Puerto Rico poured into the state looking for work.

As whites moved to the suburbs, racial tensions grew, leading to riots in the 1960s. New York Governor Nelson Rockefeller set aside funds for housing and job training for the poor. Though Rockefeller's policies were meant to help people and sometimes did, in the end they left the state poor. As a result, in 1975 New York came very close to declaring bankruptcy.

New York Today

After narrowly steering clear of financial disaster, New York has rebounded beyond anyone's wildest dreams. The excellent economy of the 1980s and 1990s brought businesses and young professionals back to the city. Rudolph Giuliani, New York's mayor from 1994 until 2001, deserves credit for adding more police to the streets and bringing the city's crime problem under control. By the mid-1990s, New York City came to be admired as an exciting place, home to creative, interesting people. Indeed, there was a new shine on the Big Apple.

On the morning of September 11, 2001, terrorists who held a strict fundamentalist view of the Islamic religion hijacked four airplanes. At 8:48 A.M. the terrorists crashed a jet plane in the top floors of the North Tower of Manhattan's famous World Trade Center's Twin Towers. A little after 9:00 A.M. the second plane crashed into the South Tower. Though some people managed to escape from the burning buildings, many weren't so lucky. By the end of the day, both enormous towers had collapsed, and more than 3,000 people were dead. Among them were 60 police officers and 343 firefighters. Along with the casualties from the third plane, which the terrorists crashed into the Pentagon (America's Department of

On September 11, 2001, hundreds of firefighters put their lives on the line to save people trapped in the World Trade Center towers.

Defense, outside Washington, D.C.), and the fourth plane, which crashed in a field near Pittsburgh, the death toll was well over twice that of Pearl Harbor—the 1941 attack on America by the Japanese that triggered America's entry into World War II.

A national tragedy, the collapse of the World Trade Towers was an even deeper wound for New York City. But out of disaster, New Yorkers bonded as never before and showed the world the unique nature of their strength and spirit. Volunteers rushed downtown to search for survivors and to help clear debris. Others lined up to donate blood. Money poured into funds to aid families of victims. The incredible bravery of the firefighters and police officers was acknowledged worldwide as was Mayor Giuliani's skillful leadership during the city's darkest days. In an address to the nation, President George W. Bush held up the badge of a stricken New York City policeman as a reminder of his personal pledge to keep America safe and to rebuild the Big Apple.

Important Dates

A.D. 700   Mound Builders from Mississippi and Ohio River Valleys spread into modern-day New York.

1524   Giovanni da Verrazano becomes the first European to sail into New York Harbor. Today a bridge is named after him.

1570   Establishment of the Iroquois Confederacy

1609   Henry Hudson sails as far as Albany, New York, up the river that will bear his name.

1626   The Dutch buy the island of Manhattan from Native Americans.

1664   The British take control of Dutch New Netherland and rename it New York.

1777   The Battle of Saratoga. A victory by the rebel forces marks a turning point in the Revolutionary War.

1785-1789   New York is America's first national capital.

1788   New York officially enters the Union as the eleventh state.

1825   The Erie Canal is completed.

Statue of Liberty

1827   Slavery is abolished in New York State.

1886   The Statue of Liberty is unveiled in New York Harbor.

1898   The five boroughs of Manhattan, Brooklyn, Queens, the Bronx, and Staten Island unite to form New York City.

1929   The stock-market crash marks the beginning of the Great Depression and one of the toughest decades in New York and American history.

1947   Jackie Robinson signs a contract with the Brooklyn Dodgers, becoming the first African American to play major-league baseball.

1952   The United Nations building opens in New York City.

1955   The Brooklyn Dodgers defeat the New York Yankees to win the World Series.

1975   A major financial crisis in the state and city

Jackie Robinson

1984   Congresswoman Geraldine Ferraro of Queens becomes the first woman to be nominated by a major political party for vice president.

1990s   Boom times increase the state budget. Mayor Rudolph Giuliani leads a campaign to reduce crime in New York City.

2001   Terrorists hijack four planes, crashing two of them into New York City's World Trade Center.

3 The People

Since the mid-1800s, New York City has served as the main entry point for immigrants into the United States. As a result, New York has become one of the most ethnically diverse states in the nation. As New York journalist Daniel J. Wakin says, "It's the unique mix of people that keeps New York State vibrant and strong."

The first major waves of European immigrants to arrive in the United States came mostly from Germany and Ireland. Escaping poverty and famine, these men and women came in such large numbers that by 1850 half the people living in New York City were foreign born. In the 1880s the city's population doubled when people from Italy and Eastern Europe came to America escaping religious persecution and looking for economic opportunity.

What makes New York so special? It's the invitation of the Statue of Liberty— give me your tired, your poor, your huddled masses who yearn to breathe free. Not restricted to English only.

—Jesse Jackson, African American clergyman and civil rights leader, 1988

Kermit the Frog makes an appearance at the Macy's Thanksgiving Day Parade, held each year in New York City. Other floats include Bullwinkle, Tweety Bird, and Bart Simpson.

Children are dressed up for the Caribbean Day Festival in Brooklyn.

The federal government established the Bureau of Immigration in 1890 and selected Ellis Island in New York Harbor as the site for the Federal Immigration Center. During its peak years, from 1892-1924, Ellis Island was the port of entry to America for hundreds of thousands of immigrants.

Today various ethnic groups are still flooding into the entire state. Since 1980, over 400,000 Russian Jews have moved to the Big Apple! New York City has also become the home of people from the Caribbean, Asia, and Central America.

As a result of these tidal waves of immigration, New York City is home to practically every religion and nationality in the world. Are you in the mood for Chinese food? Easy—take the downtown train to Chinatown. Feel like a cannoli afterward for dessert? Stroll across town to Little Italy. Indian food? No problem. Any native will tell you: head to Sixth Street between First and Second Avenues. You'll find thirty Indian restaurants lining the street. Or take the train uptown to Harlem, home of some of the best barbecue and old style southern-cooking restaurants in the country. Of course, you don't have to go to a specific area of town to sample different cultures. There are Chinese, Thai, Indian, Vietnamese, and Italian groceries and restaurants all over New York—most likely within a five-minute walk of your apartment! There are synagogues and churches and mosques throughout the city too.

> *Central Park is the only place on earth where you can come face to face with the whole human experience in a few square feet. There are people playing ball, people falling in love, people lying there homeless, people doing magic, people playing music, people from all over the world taking it all in. I love it.*
>
> **—Billy Aronson, author of the play Light Years and creator of the original concept and additional lyrics for the musical Rent.**

City People

"Fast-talking," "pushy," "hurried"—all of these adjectives and many more have been used to describe the typical resident of New York City. And like all stereotypes, it is partly true. Compared to many people from other states, most New Yorkers move quickly, seemingly in a hurry to get somewhere. In the process, they might brush someone on the street or get impatient while they wait at a deli for a cup of coffee. But

Ice skating at Central Park's Wollman Rink. For those who don't like the cold, the rink offers in-line skating in the summer.

this negative view is only part of the picture. An equally valid description of a typical New Yorker might be: "smart," "kind," "witty," and "caring." As one native put it, "Deep down New Yorkers are extremely nice. Always willing to give directions or lend a helping hand. Just in a hurry."

Why the big rush? The answer could lie in the lyrics to a song made popular by Frank Sinatra in the 1970s: "If I can make it there, I'll make it any-where." Most who choose to settle in New York are ambitious—whether to make it on Broadway or make a killing on Wall Street. As Moss Hart, the Pulitzer Prize–winning playwright said, "The only credential the city asked was the boldness to dream. For those who did, it unlocked its gates and treasures, not caring who they were or where they came from."

> *One of the things that amazes me is the energy that's in New York. You get no energy from the earth because the earth is all covered up with cement and bricks. . . . The energy all comes from human beings.*
>
> **—Phil Jackson, coach of the Los Angeles Lakers and former player with the New York Knicks.**

Due to its attraction to people with the "boldness to dream," New York City has become one of the leading cultural centers of the world. Spend a day in the Big Apple—there's so much to do it can be hard to know where to begin. You might go to the Museum of Modern Art in the morning, then walk over to Times Square and see a matinee of a Broadway show. Afterward, you could stroll through Central Park, grab a bite to eat, then head over to The Lincoln Center for the Performing Arts to listen to the New York Philharmonic. If you decide to stay another day or two, there is the ballet, the opera, and the art galleries, as well as more world class museums and theater.

As Madeleine Hyde, a native New Yorker and teacher, puts it: "Come to New York. Whatever you want, we've got it."

Famous New Yorkers

Franklin D. Roosevelt:
United States President

Franklin D. Roosevelt was born in 1882 in Hyde Park, New York. President of the United States from 1933 until his death in 1945, Roosevelt helped steer the country through the Great Depression and World War II. Known for his compassionate leadership, he assured a troubled nation in his first inaugural address in 1933, "The only thing we have to fear is fear itself." In 1941, after the Japanese bombed Pearl Harbor, Roosevelt called the country to arms, saying, "This is a day that will forever live in infamy!"

Eleanor Roosevelt:
First Lady

Born in 1884 in New York City, Eleanor Roosevelt married her cousin (future president Franklin Roosevelt) and then used her position as first lady to become perhaps the most influential woman of the twentieth century. She was an author, and a humanitarian. Roosevelt taught at a school set up for poor children and helped run a factory for jobless farmers in the winter. As she put it, "You get more joy out of giving to others, and should put a good deal of thought into the happiness you are able to give."

Woody Allen: Filmmaker

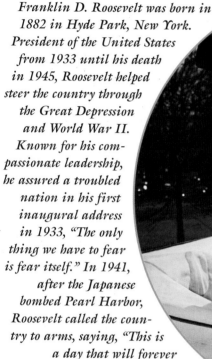

Allan Stewart Konigsberg was born in 1935 and raised in Brooklyn. He later changed his name to Woody Allen and became one of the most important comic filmmakers of his generation. Most of his many movies, like Hannah and her Sisters, Manhattan, *and* Broadway Danny Rose, *celebrate and gently mock city life. Making a career out of playing a neurotic New Yorker, Allen's life view might be best summed up by the opening lines of* Annie Hall, *one of his most famous films. "There's an old joke," says Allen to the camera. "Two elderly women are at a Catskills mountain resort, and one of them says, 'Boy, the food at this place is really terrible.' The other one says, 'Yeah, I know, and such small portions.'"*

Shirley Chisholm: Congresswoman

Born in Brooklyn in 1924, Shirley Chisholm became in 1968 the first African-American woman to be a member of Congress, running on the slogan, "Fighting Shirley Chisholm—Unbought and Unbossed." During her first term, she hired an all-female staff and spoke out for civil rights and against the war in Vietnam. She said, "Women in this country must refuse to accept the old, the traditional roles and stereotypes." In 1972, Chisholm became the first black woman to mount a serious campaign for the Democratic Party's nomination for president. She retired from Congress in 1982. In June 2001, the United States House of Representatives honored her enduring achievements and contributions to her country by a unanimous 415-0 vote.

Joe DiMaggio: Baseball Player

The New York Yankees' Joe DiMaggio was one of the greatest baseball players of his era. In his career, which stretched from 1936 to 1951, DiMaggio was named the American League's Most Valuable Player three times. In 1941, he hit safely in fifty-six consecutive games, one of the longest-standing records in modern baseball.

"I can describe Joe in one word: class," said Pete Sheehy, former Yankee clubhouse manager. "He was the most perfect ballplayer I ever saw, but he was a shy fellow. I'll tell you something else though. When Joe DiMaggio walks into the clubhouse, the lights flicker. He's the star."

Langston Hughes: Author

One of America's foremost writers, Langston Hughes was born in Joplin, Missouri, in 1902 but moved to Harlem in 1924. From the 1920s through the 1960s Hughes devoted his life to writing novels, short stories, plays, and poems that dramatized the black American experience.

Let America be America again—
The land that never has been yet—
And yet must be—the land where every man is free,
The land that's mine—the poor man's, Indian's, Negro's,
ME—
Who made America,
Whose seat and blood, whose faith and pain,
Whose hand at the foundry, whose plow in the rain
Must bring back our mighty dream again.

—LANGSTON HUGHES, "LET AMERICA BE AMERICA AGAIN"

Upstate Pride

The state of New York is largely divided into three groups: the city dwellers; those who prefer a home and yard in the suburbs but still want to be close enough to a city to take advantage of what it has to offer; and finally, those New Yorkers who enjoy the pleasures of small-town rural life.

Though New York State is home to several major cities, most of the state is made up of smaller communities that are throwbacks to an earlier era. Many upstaters feel that what they lack in excitement and ethnic diversity they make up for in community. As Matthew Benson—a photographer and long-time Manhattanite turned upstate resident—says, "In the city you're living on top of and beside other people. The sidewalk is a communal area. In the country, you have your own house, your own yard. . . you can walk out onto your own grass and have a sense of your own space."

A moment of discovery in the autumn leaves

Making Butter

New York settlers raised cows for milk, butter, and cheese. You can make butter with a lightweight modern "churn"—a water bottle.

What You Need

1/2 pint whipping cream
Clean, empty plastic water bottle with cap—
    about 25 fluid ounce size
Funnel (optional)
3 clean glass marbles
Bowl
Dash of salt—about 1/8 teaspoon (optional)

Leave the cream out of the refrigerator until it comes to room temperature (60–90 minutes, but no more than 2 hours for safety reasons). Pour into bottle (a funnel can help), add marbles, and cap tightly.

Shake bottle vigorously for 5 to 10 minutes. It's fun to do this with a friend. After a few minutes, the marbles will stop banging. If you stop now, you'll have thick whipped cream. Keep shaking another 5 minutes or so, until you can see and hear a large solid lump moving inside the bottle. That's butter.

Squeeze the bottle over the bowl like you'd squeeze a tube of toothpaste. You may need to cut the bottle to reclaim your marbles.

Knead the butter with clean hands and pour out any extra liquid. Work in salt if you like. Keep your finished butter in the refrigerator.

Try some! It's good!

And residents of New York's great upstate cities take great pride in their home towns as well. Says Buffalo resident Mo Ganey, "Everyone here considers it a civic responsibility to root for the Bills. The day Buffalo lost to the Giants in the Super Bowl in 1991 on a final missed field goal was the worst day for the city since President McKinley was assassinated!" And well-known newscaster Tim Russert has said, "You can take the boy out of Buffalo. But you can't take Buffalo out of the boy."

An estimated 75,000 gallons of water per second flow over Niagara's towering American Falls! Geologists predict that water erosion on the soft shale and limestone will cause the falls to change over time into a series of descending rapids.

Aside from sports, the people of Buffalo are proud of the beautiful old stone houses with large porches that line their city streets—not to mention the five homes designed by world famous architect Frank Lloyd Wright. In Rochester, the citizens are proud of being called the image capital, home to Xerox and Eastman Kodak. Many citizens enjoy taking walks along the Erie Canal at night. Residents are also proud of the city's history of social consciousness. Susan B. Anthony, who fought for women's voting rights, lived in Rochester. And Frederick Douglass, the great African American who fought to free slaves, is buried in the city where he lived and gave many of his most rousing speeches. Says Rachel Halling, a teacher in Rochester, "The cities of Western New York have a lot to offer in the way of arts and culture. We also have a broad cross

A grandfather and his grandson set out for an afternoon of fishing on one of New York State's many beautiful lakes.

The University of Rochester's Eastman School of Music, established in 1921 by George Eastman, founder of the Eastman Kodak Company, is now known as one of the foremost music conservatories in the world. The school schedules and supports over seven hundred concerts a year.

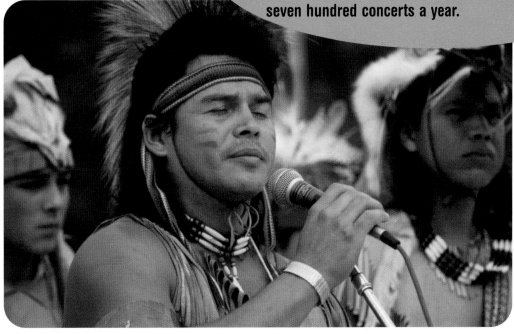

A Native American in the town of Woodstock demonstrates a traditional song.

The People

Built during the depression, the Empire State Building was the tallest building in the world for many years.

New York

section of people up here—all ethnic groups, all religions. We aren't intimidated by New York City—no way!"

Crime

For years tourists visiting Manhattan were told: "Don't go outside at night. You'll be mugged!" Though crime in the city was never that bad, it is true that the people of New York's cities have grappled with rising crime rates for years. In the 1980s, the emergence of a powerful drug known as crack contributed to rising robbery and murder rates throughout the state. Crime became such a pressing issue that an ex-federal prosecutor, Rudolph Giuliani, ran for mayor of New York City in 1993, vowing to clean up the streets. By hiring more police, especially in high-crime neighborhoods, Mayor Giuliani caused New York City's crime rates to drop drastically. Though the mayor was criticized for being too aggressive in some of his tactics, most New Yorkers rightfully believed their neighborhoods were safer.

New Yorkers have waged a war against crime on the state level too. According to the United States Department of Justice, violent crime is down 28 percent statewide. Statistics from 1994 to 1997 show robberies down 35 percent and murder down by nearly half!

All of this is good news for New York. For years the Empire State was burdened by a reputation for a high crime rate. With safer streets and a strong economy, tourism in the 1990s skyrocketed. More and more people from all over the world came to visit the Empire State—to see a Broadway show in New York City, or hear the Buffalo Philharmonic, or to go to the National Women's Hall of Fame in Seneca Falls.

Calendar of Events

Adirondack National Car Show in Lake George

Every September at the park in Fort William Henry, owners of classic automobiles gather and take a drive through town.

The Americade in Lake George

Each year in early June, 50,000-60,000 motorcyclists drive through town and show off their machines.

Free Concerts in New York City

All summer long the New York Philharmonic and Metropolitan Opera give free concerts in the parks of New York City.

Shakespeare in the Park

Each summer at the Delacorte Theater in Central Park, Shakespeare's and other great plays are performed for free.

Renaissance Festival in Sterling

A re-creation of a typical English festival in the Renaissance featuring actors dressed in period costumes is held from early July through mid-August. There are lots of fun activities for kids.

Celebration of the Chinese New Year

Niagara Canal Fest in North Tonawanda

This eight-day festival held every July in honor of the Erie Canal features fishing contests, rubber-duck races, chain-saw carving, and concerts by the Buffalo Philharmonic.

A New York State Fair

Niagara's Pirates Festival in Olcott

Each July, visitors to this festival dress up as pirates, fight water wars with balloons, and search for buried treasure.

New York State Fair in Syracuse

Held during the last few weeks of August through Labor Day, this fair includes rides, exhibits, food, and concerts.

Columbia County Fair in Chatham

Held in early September for 164 years, this is the oldest agricultural fair in the state. There are rides, booths, exhibits, and animal shows and competitions.

Peach Festival in Lewiston

This annual festival held in early September features food and games, as well as contests related to the peach: Peach Queen, Peach Blossom, and Peach Fuzz.

World's Largest Garage Sale in Warrensburg, Warren County

Every year around the end of September or early October, the town of Warrensburg is closed off to let thousands of people set up shop for one big sale. Some residents also participate, selling from tables in their front yards.

A gift from the French government,
The Statue of Liberty was unveiled in
New York Bay in 1886.

4 How It Works

When New York governor George Pataki gave his State of the State Address on January 3, 2001, he began by saying: "It's an honor to once again report on the state of the State. And it is a pleasure for me to be able to report that our State is strong, and our future bright with possibilities."

Though it is the job of most politicians to put a positive spin on their big speeches, Governor Pataki has reason to feel optimistic about New York's future. Even so, there are many difficult issues that he and the New York senate and assembly must face if New York's future is to remain as bright as its past.

How New York Votes

For years, statewide elections in New York split evenly: upstate voters favored Republicans while the city folks pulled the voting levers for Democrats. But recently, the slowdown in manufacturing has caused a million upstaters to move in search of jobs. At the same time, there has been a huge migration from New York's cities. As a result, the politics of the state have shifted. Today Democrats outnumber Republicans by a ratio of 5 to 3. Or as Skip Wilkens, an English teacher from White Plains, put it: "In New York statewide elections, a Democratic politician rolls

55

out of bed with a million more votes than his Republican opponent."

One of the challenges of governing a state like New York is balancing the needs of the residents of its cities with those in rural communities. "Drive through a town like Whitehall," says John Buck, longtime New York resident. "It's small and rural-almost like Vermont. Sometimes it's hard

Boys bike past Tibbitts Point Lighthouse, at the mouth of the Saint Lawrence River on Lake Ontario.

to believe that we vote for the same governor as the people in the big city." New York's elected representatives must work hard to make sure that every citizen gets a fair shake.

Making a Bill a Law

Like any government, the senators and assemblymen of New York have to work together to solve statewide problems. Though Republicans and Democrats often disagree about the correct way to attack a problem, they are ultimately faced with a choice: compromise or get nothing done. And New York government is all about compromise. Despite the increase in the number of Democrats in the state, New York's senate is

Branches of Government

Executive The chief executive officer of the state, New York's governor is elected to a four-year term and is responsible for appointing judges, drawing up the budget, and introducing legislation he would like to see enacted into law.

Legislative Like most other states (and the federal government), New York's law-makers are divided into two houses: the senate with 61 members and the assembly with 150 members, all elected to two-year terms. The legislators can pass a law by a simple majority vote in both houses but need a two-thirds vote to override a governor's veto.

Judicial New York's highest court, the court of appeals, is made up of a chief justice and six associates, all appointed to fourteen-year terms. The next-highest court, the appellate, mostly hears appeals from lower courts. Its justices are appointed by the governor. The supreme court is New York's lowest court. Justices are elected to fourteen-year terms.

still controlled by Republicans. On the other hand, its state assembly has been under Democratic control since 1974! As a result, the leaders of these two houses, the senate majority leader and the speaker of the assembly (in 2001, Joseph L. Bruno and Sheldon Silver respectively), have come to wield enormous power. Not only do these two men decide what's voted on in their houses, they often negotiate directly with the governor. This way of operating causes some critics to refer to New York government as three men in a room. Though the senate majority leader and the speaker of the assembly always need the votes of their members in the

Statues honoring our nation's history can be found throughout the state. This statue of General Philip Sheridan stands in front of the New York State Capitol. Born in Albany, he fought in the Civil War and later served as the commanding general of the United States Army.

legislature to pass a bill, their influence is so enormous that when they and the governor agree to do something, it is almost certain to happen.

Since the senate and the assembly have been controlled by opposing parties for so many years, New York's government is set up for cutting deals. For example, in 1997 the governor and the Republicans in the senate wanted to pass a certain tax cut. In order to get the assembly to go along with it, the Republicans agreed to support a series of education programs favored by the Democrats. As a worker in Albany (New York's capital) put it, "Getting laws passed here is all about horse trading."

Of course, not all the power lies with the leaders of the two houses and the governor. Most new bills start with a single senator or assembly member who introduces his or her idea to his chamber of the legislature. Once the idea for the bill is introduced it is referred to a standing committee for debate. At this point the bill can be rejected. But if a majority of committee members support the new bill the full senate or assembly can debate and vote on the issue. If the bill still gets a majority vote, it is passed to the other legislative house, which will then debate its merits. But the bill's journey to becoming a law isn't over yet! Even if a bill is popular, the senate and the assembly often come up with different versions. These need to be ironed out in a committee. When the senate and the assembly finally agree on the details and wording of the bill, they send it to the governor for his signature. Of course, if the governor doesn't like the bill he can veto it. Since the mid-1970s neither house of the legislature has had the two-thirds vote needed to override a veto. This makes the New York governor extremely powerful.

Education

As New York faces the twenty-first century, its lawmakers definitely have their work cut out for them. "The biggest problem facing New York State is how to fix the public education system," state senator Eric Schneiderman says. "A substantial number of kids are nowhere near reading level. If you don't have a trained workforce you can't compete in the global economy."

Many New Yorkers complain that public schools aren't geting enough funding from the state. Others see problems not so much with the total amount of state funding as with the way that funding is distributed. Early in 2001, a New York Supreme Court justice, Leland DeGrasse, ruled that the state's formula for divvying up money among different districts was racially biased. Judge DeGrasse ruled that the state had to come up with ways to give more money to New York City schools, which have largely African American, Hispanic, and Asian student bodies. Governor Pataki's administration has argued for a reversal of Judge DeGrasse's ruling, but many New Yorkers, especially leaders of minority groups in the city, believe the ruling should stand.

Some New Yorkers, mostly residents of wealthy communities, have a different complaint. They feel that the state's requirement that students pass a series of exams before heading on to high schools should apply only to school districts that are doing poorly.

New York is a long way from having an educational system that will meet the demands of all of its residents completely.

What You Can Do

In a state as large as New York, people sometimes feel that they have no power to affect their government. In fact, that isn't true. "There are lots of ways to get involved," says Senator Schneiderman. "You can work for a community agency. Or contact your elected officials. If I get a hundred phone calls about a certain issue, that issue is high up on my radar screen."

Young people can make a difference. In 1998, the deputy campaign manager for Eric Schneiderman's senate bid was David Gringer, an eleventh grader at Stuyvesant High School in New York City. His assistant was Micah Lasher—a tenth grader! "Campaigns are always looking for people to help out," a New York community board member said. "Just show up and start stuffing envelopes."

Of course, even if you aren't interested in full-time involvement you can keep up to date by reading one of New York's excellent newspapers or by scanning the Internet. Or you can form a political club. Recently, a group of five ten-year-olds in the fourth grade at the Dalton School in New York City did just that, forming a society they call D-PAK or "Democratically Politically Active Kids." Meeting for two hours every five weeks, the members of D-PAK discuss politics over pizza and potato chips. "By our bylaws," says Sarah Gitlin, "anyone who's a Democrat who's under eighteen can join." One meeting featured Larry Kramer, a New York University law professor, discussing the Supreme Court's involvement in the 2000 national election.

Here are two websites you can visit if you want to e-mail your state representatives.
To find an e-mail address for a New York State senator visit: www.senate.state.ny.us/senate.html Click on "Senate E-mail Addresses."
To find an e-mail address for a member of the New York assembly visit: http://assembly.state.ny.us Select "Assembly Members" and then select the person to whom you want to write.

Who knows? Perhaps the young members of D-PAK will one day be the senators, assemblymen, and governors of the state.

A young farmer brings a giant pumpkin to a market.

5 Making a Living

New York State has enjoyed a history of great economic success. Since New York Harbor was a natural entry port into the New World, it didn't take long for Manhattan to become the financial center of the world. And after the completion of the Erie Canal, the city's wealth spread to Rochester, Syracuse, Buffalo, and other cities, towns, and farms that dot the northern and western sections of the state. But despite an impressive record of economic growth, New York State faces some tough challenges as it looks toward the twenty-first century.

New York is the world leader in the financial services industry. Nearly every major investment bank and brokerage firm has an office in Manhattan—many in the Wall Street district. And during the 1990s, New York's financial businesses went through the roof, accounting for about a quarter of the state's dollars. New York State enjoys many vital agricultural businesses. The state has about 32,000 farms and is the third

> There's no denying that New York City can be an expensive place to live. As Jack Barry, entertainer and game-show host, said: "The trouble with New York is it's so convenient to everything I can't afford."

New York State is home to hundreds of vineyards.

New York

largest producer of milk and other dairy products in the nation, behind California and Wisconsin. Apple orchards and vineyards dot the state. New York is also well known for its livestock. Farmers raise beef cattle, hogs, and sheep. The Empire State is also responsible for producing millions of chickens and eggs every year.

In 1999, the combined sales value of New York turkeys, ducks, eggs, and chickens was just under $57 million!

Recently a new kind of business has come to New York. The nationwide economic expansion of the 1990s brought enormous growth in dot.com companies. But then came a sudden downturn. The NASDAQ (the economic standard used to measure technology companies) dropped by more than 50 percent in 2000 and 2001! Still, many New Yorkers place their faith in the future of technology.

Products & Resources

Apples

In 1600, European settlers brought dried apple seeds with them to plant in New York. Today New York is one of the leading producers of apples in the country.

The Theater

New York City is the home of Broadway, the world's largest theater district. Musicals and plays such as The Producers and Proof bring countless tourist dollars to the city each year.

Dairy Farms

New York State has 8,000 dairy farms, most of them family owned and operated.

Publishing

New York leads the nation in the production of books, newspapers, and magazines. New York has fifty-six daily newspapers, including The New York Times *and* The Wall Street Journal, *which are distributed internationally.*

Finance

New York City is the hub of the world's financial network. Virtually every important business related to the financial services industry has offices in midtown Manhattan or in the Wall Street area.

Transportation

Though airplanes and railroads are now key methods of transport, the Erie Canal still pulls its weight, moving goods from New York to the Midwest.

Problems Upstate

Though New York's financial industries have thrived and agriculture has held it's own, the economic outlook isn't nearly as rosy for upstate manufacturing businesses. According to the 2000 census, over one million people moved from northern and western New York between 1990 and 2000, usually in search of better jobs.

"It's a serious problem," says New York writer, Eric Weiner. "To lure people back, we need to invest in the infrastructure of these communities and make sure that there are good transportation and public schools. The things that attract and keep businesses."

Governor Pataki and the state legislature are doing what they can to lure new businesses to the region. In recent years they have created "Empire Zones," a series of districts throughout the state in which businesses that create jobs can receive tax breaks. Still, it is an upward climb. As new technologies take the place of old industries, like steel manufacturing, some businesses are simply getting phased

Two girls eat ice cream cones on Wellesley Island, a vacation community in Thousand Islands.

out. Even old reliables like Xerox in Rochester are struggling.

Though tax incentives are one way to get upstate business rolling again, some upstate communities are taking matters into their own hands.

Republican governor Pataki has taken credit for generating half a million jobs in New York since 1995. But Democratic state assembly speaker Sheldon Silver says, "If New York had grown as fast as other states like Florida, Texas, or California, we would have generated more than one million new jobs." Another example of politics at work in New York.

In Rochester, for example, residents have long been divided over a proposal aimed at boosting tourism by expanding their city's zoo, the Seneca Park Zoo. One faction, led by Republican County Executive Jack D. Doyle, sees the zoo's expansion as a quick and easy way to help the city's depressed economy. But to build a zoo on the scale Doyle proposes, it would be necessary to tear up much of historic Seneca Park—a park designed by Frederick Olmsted, the famous landscaper responsible for New York City's Central and Prospect Park.

"They want to tear up the park and put in a giant parking lot," says one Rochester resident. "A lot of people don't want that." In fact, there is a movement in Rochester called SOS, standing for Save Our Seneca Parks.

Just because the proposed expansion of the Seneca Park Zoo is a local issue does not mean deciding on it will be easy.

The Budget

"It may sound dull," says reporter Peter French, "but the most important thing the legislature does every year is pass the budget. And the budget often dictates statewide economic policy."

That is undoubtedly true. How it works is this: In January of each year, the governor submits what he thinks the budget for the following year should be, giving weight to his own priorities. It is generally assumed that this first figure will be a starting point and that the senate and the assembly will insist upon more money to fund their own specific pet projects. But this is where the fun begins. Usually, the senate Republicans

A tourist ship docks in New York Harbor. The Big Apple remains one of the most exciting places to visit in the world.

want to spend the state's money differently than the Democrats in the assembly!

For instance, in 2001 the boom of the 1990s seemed to be over. Given the uncertainty of the country's economic outlook, Governor Pataki decided that it would be reckless for the state

A boy gets a close-up look at a statue at the Metropolitan Museum of Art in New York City. The cost of running the city's many museums comes largely from its budget.

to go on a spending binge. He proposed a budget of 83.4 billion dollars—a 6 percent increase over previous years.

Too bad the two houses of the legislature weren't satisfied. The Republicans in the senate wanted about half a billion more to fund biotech projects, education, and non-profit organizations. The Democrats in the assembly demanded that 2 billion be added to the budget, largely for education. With the three bodies of the government holding different views, it was time for negotiation. But the state constitution states that New York's budget has to be finished by April 1. (Most other state budgets don't have to be completed until mid-summer.) As a result, the budget didn't pass on time. Not that this was unusual. New York's budget hasn't passed on time for the past seventeen years!

"They always seem to get it done," said Peter French. "It just takes the governor, the senate, and the assembly a long time to figure out the nuts and bolts and cut the deal."

In this way, New York's economic policy is often affected by politics. Let's say the upstate Republican senators want more money to help small businesses get started and the city Democrats want more money for schools. A deal might be

Making a Living

negotiated in which the Republicans and Democrats vote for what the others want in order to get money for their own constituents.

It may not be perfect—but that's how government and economic policy often work in New York.

Environmental Concerns

In the mid-1830s, the New York State Legislature realized that it had to do something to ensure that New York City would have clean water for years to come. Its solution was to grant the city the authority to build aqueducts, series of underground tunnels that carried water through Westchester County. The first aqueduct was completed and put into service in 1842. In the early 1900s that series of aqueducts was expanded to include land in the Catskills. Then the legislature gave the city the right to purchase more land as its water needs grew. Modern-day New Yorkers benefit greatly from the foresight of politicians from an earlier day.

"One of the reasons that New York State has prospered has been its visionary investments in its future," says lawyer Jonathan Hanning. "One of those is the New York watersheds [reservoirs of clean water]."

Though a real success, the upstate watersheds policy has raised an important environmental issue: how to balance the city's need for clean water with their upstate neighbors' desire for economic development. Recently some citizens of New York's rural communities decided not to sell their land to the city, preferring to use it themselves to build homes and start businesses. To make matters worse for the Big Apple, upstate construction can create pollutants that run into the city's valuable water supply.

A quiet lake in the Adirondacks

In 1992, a New York City Agency called the Department of Environmental Protection, or simply the DEP, began to work with upstate farms, many of them dairy farms, in a voluntary program offering them funds and assistance to make their farms more environmentally sound. "The hope, of course," says Larry Beckhardt, program director, "is that cleaner farms will eventually lead to a cleaner environment and cleaner water for the city."

In the past ten years, the DEP has helped many farms run more efficiently and at a greater profit. "We've done a lot of good things," Beckhardt says. "But whether that shows up down the line in cleaner water samples? It's too early to tell."

Again, the needs of the city and upstate had to be balanced and considered. In 1997, Governor Pataki negotiated an agreement called the Watershed Memorandum of Agreement that forced the city to pay upstate towns for use of their land. It was an effort to address the upstaters' economic needs while allowing city residents access to clean water.

New York Faces the Twenty-first Century

"The attack on the World Trade Center was a tragedy," says Dora Barton, a New York science teacher. "But the spirit of the New York people rose like a thunderbolt out of the ashes. Firemen, cops, people on the street—everyone rose to the challenge and made the city proud."

As New York faces the new millennium, it can take strength from the reaction of its people to the horrific events of September 11, 2001. No doubt about it: New Yorkers can take a punch. And they have made it absolutely clear that they will work together to meet every challenge.

Within weeks of the attack, there were proposals on the table to rebuild New York City's financial district. The area around the World Trade Center was blocked off and began to be cleared. People went back to work. The city's upstate neighbors held prayer vigils and fund drives to show their support for the Big Apple. Joined as one by a tragedy, the people of New York proved that the spirit of their forefathers, who worked so hard to build the Erie Canal, was still alive. Yes, New York is a state of vibrant cities and stunning beauty, but most would agree that its people remain its greatest natural resource.

New York

A Statue of Liberty look-alike collects donations for families of victims of the September 11 attack on the Twin Towers.

Making a Living

New York's flag shows the state's coat of arms against a dark blue background. The coat of arms is made up of a sunrise, a three-masted ship, and a Hudson River sloop within a shield. An eagle is perched on a globe above the shield. Below is the state's motto, Excelsior [Ever Upward]. On either side of the shield stand figures representing Liberty and Justice.

More About New York

Books

About the State

Capstone Press, Geography Department Staff. *New York*. Mankato, MN: Capstone Press, 1996.

Fradin, Dennis B. *New York*. Danbury, CT: Children's Press, 2003.

Thompson, Kathleen. *New York*. Austin, TX: Raintree Steck-Vaughn, 1996.

About New York City

Davis, James E. and Sharryl Davis Hawke. *New York City*. Milwaukee, WI: Raintree Publishers, 1990.

Hatt, Christine. *New York*. Mankato, MN: Thameside Press, 2000.

Kent, Deborah. *New York City*. Danbury, CT: Children's Press, 1996.

Tagliaferro, Linda. *Destination New York*. Minneapolis, MN: Lerner Publications, 1998.

Of Special Interest

Fisher, Leonard Everett. *Ellis Island: Gateway to the New World*. New York: Holiday House, 1986.

Lourie, Peter. *Erie Canal: Canoeing America's Great Waterway*. Honesdale, PA: Boyds Mills Press, 1997.

McNeese, Tim. *The New York Subway System*. San Diego, CA: Lucent Books, 1997.

Websites

Learning Adventures in Citizenship: From New York to Your Town
(Web companion to PBS series *New York: A Documentary Film*):
http://www.pbs.org/wnet/newyork/laic

Official New York State Tourism Website: http://iloveny.state.ny.us/

Get the Facts About New York State: (NYS Department of State):
http://www.dos.state.ny.us/kidsroom/nysfacts/factmenu.html

New York State Homepage: http://www.state.ny.us/

About the Author

Dan Elish is the author of numerous books for children, including histories of
the transcontinental railroad and the Cherokee Trail of Tears. He has also
written several novels for young readers, including *The Worldwide Dessert
Contest*, *The Great Squirrel Uprising*, *Born Too Short*, and *Confessions of an 8th
Grade Basket Case*, as well as several musicals. He lives in New York City.

Index

Page numbers in **boldface** are illustrations.